Beyond *My* Wounds

Prophetess
Nicole Haynes

ISBN 979-8-88616-529-6 (paperback)
ISBN 979-8-88616-530-2 (digital)

Christian Faith Publishing
832 Park Avenue
Meadville, PA 16335
www.christianfaithpublishing.com

Bible verses that is being used in reference in the book is The King James Bible Version

Printed in the United States of America

Contents

Acknowledgment

In dedication first to my Lord and Savior, Jesus Christ. To the Trinity of God, God the Father, God the Son, and God the Holy Spirit, in whom without I am nothing! To God be the praise, honor, and the glory.

This dedication comes with the power of God that through and in His Son, Jesus Christ, you, too, can be set free, as I was, from drugs, alcoholism, nicotine, molestation, rejection, oppression, and depression.

(Can you shout with me and say, "I BREAK ITS POWER!")

To my beautiful daughters, Keairra and Keanna Haynes, in which God blessed me, who have had a major impact on my journey of *Beyond My Wounds*. Spiritually, the motivation was from God, in birth of my daughters, to stop the generations of curse so that it did not pass down to them.

To my husband, MacDonald Haynes, whose hands played a great part in assisting and helping me along in life, who has been faithful and patient, trusting the power of God in my life.

Foreword

Beyond My Wounds is a helpful study for anyone desiring to grow in their spiritual and natural walk in life. The guidance provided in this book will enhance your spiritual insight to be able to decern the current activities of the demon that will try to impose itself against your God-given rights, authority, and freedom. You will be enhanced in the knowledge of the enemy activities against your life and discover the answer to the most common questions people ask concerning their healing process.

The Introduction

Better days is what Job 8:7 describes in the scripture, "Though thy beginning was small, yet thy latter end shall greatly increase." Yes! You are about to embark on a journey that will lead you to your freedom. I said "yes" as I was speaking to your spiritual man, for there is a desire to get beyond your wounds, to obtain and possess your later blessing.

Getting *beyond your wounds*. Breaking the power of your wounds as God begins to lead you on this journey of spiritual healing and deliverance where you are free according to John 8:36, "If the Son therefore shall make you free, you shall be free indeed." In this journey, I am a strong believer that we have power in our tongue and that there is a supernatural power in which God has given us. So you will see me say, "Put this in the atmosphere." At that very moment, stop and begin to open up your mouth and release whatever is being asked of you. We have to understand that death and life is in the power of our tongues (Proverbs 18:21). Notice that when we quote this scripture, we always say "life and death is in the power of the tongue."

However, life is rarely spoken first when obstacles arise in our life, or as the scripture says, "When trouble or persecution comes because of the word sake, immediately we are offended" (Mark 4:17). In most instances, we at first get angry, allowing sin to enter in, giving it full control of that moment and time. Once sin has entered in, according to the Word of God, it then brings forth death and damnation. You have an enemy (Satan) whose main purpose since the time you came out of the birth canal was to stop the plan of God on your life. What better way to do this than to wound you so that he can steal, kill, and destroy the destiny of God from your life (John 10:10)? Well, you might say, "That's not me, and my life is not that bad."

The Word of God says, "I come to give you LIFE and that more abundantly." Ask yourself the questions below:

1. Do I really have life in all areas of my life? Think about it.
2. Do I still feel pain symptoms from the wound that was inflicted ten, fifteen, or twenty years ago?
3. Does the enemy throw fiery darts that cause me to be reminded of the past wound, having my mindset to be drawn back to the original setting in which the wound took place? Leaving me now futureless (stuck in the past) in my mind and my hopes?

Is this you? If so, come, let's go on a spiritual journey where your wounds will no longer have power or dominion over you.

(Speak this in the atmosphere.)

I break the power of my wounds in Jesus's name.

I am a living witness of many inflicted wounds and how I overcame them by the power of God. Now I can truly live the life in which God has ordained for me. A life full of the abundance of God's grace and supernatural natural favor.

Note

____

____

____

____

Chapter

2

The Knowledge of the Wounds

In order to gain power over anything, you first must understand the source of its originations. Why does it exist? What is its purpose? And, finally, what is the outcome? A weapon that is formed "comes into existence" as an enemy of war. Remember, the purpose of a weapon is to cause spiritual and bodily harm. The last and the final end result of a weapon is to destroy and kill. However, we do have hope knowing that the Word of God says in Isaiah 54:17, "No weapon that is formed shall be able to prosper." Meaning that its intended outcome is unsuccessful.

Let's take a look at a wound from a medical standpoint. We know once a wound has been inflicted, whether it is internal or external, that it must be attended to immediately. If it's just a minor cut or scrape, we will usually apply some kind of ointment and then a bandage on it. If it is major, one will go to the hospital, and surgical attention may be needed for its healing process to begin. Notice that as soon as a natural wound has come into existence, the first thing the physician begins to do is clean the wound. Why? Because the power source of an unattended wound is to cause infection.

If an infection is not treated with the proper antibiotic, then that infection can lead to a series of problems, which could lead to the possibility of death. If you had a wound of any sort such as molestation, abuse, neglect, rape, abandonment, or loss of loved one, and it did not get immediate attention to break its power, you probably have been infected by its power source.

This is where Satan captures the people of God. Since the majority of our wounds were inflicted when we were babies, children, teenagers, or young adults, these inflictions came to us at a vulnerable stage (time) in our life, and since such immediate attention was not dealt with or applied to the wounds, now it has become infected. This lets us know when God has a calling on our life, that the first attack of the enemy is to afflict us at a vulnerable stage in our life. This is seen when Jesus was born and how King Herod sought to kill Him as a baby (Matthew 2:1–16).

Know that it is a sure fact if one's not careful, then the enemy will cause spiritual blindness to those who God has chosen to watch over you, cover you, and protect you so that they could not recognize or stop the hit before it happens. These people are usually mothers, fathers, aunties, uncles, etc. We then retaliate against them, which is the second assignment of the enemy to bring about separation because we are led to believe in our own mind that if it wasn't for their ignorance, lack of proper care, and lack of love for us, then that which happened could have been prevented. When in actuality, they, too, were spiritually blinded to the real attack, which originated in the spiritual realm first and then manifested in the natural realm.

We see this similar scenario in 2 Samuel 13:1–36. Here we see how King David's daughter, Tamar, was raped by her own brother, Amnon, who the enemy blinded with the spirit of lust. These acts induced by the enemy brought on shame, incest, murder, and family disputes against David and his sons, Amnon and Absalom.

You may ask the question, how do I know that I've been affected by my past wounds? Most wounds are covered up until the cares of this life bears its weight on you. It is actually at those times that you're reminded of the past hurt and label it as the source of your life's problem and the reason life did not give you the better hand. If so, you have been infected by your wound. Now don't get me wrong, we all have experienced good days and bad days, but your bad day should not take you to a dark place of no hope.

This is why it is so important that you get beyond your wounds. It's time to get to a place that you no longer have the mindset of wanting to give up. It's time to get to a place where you break the feeling of the merry-go-round of cycles and pain that repetitively show up year after year. It's time that you no longer allow the pain of your past to choke the life out of you. Luke 10:19 reads, "Behold I give you power to tread on serpents and scorpions, and over all the power of the enemy: and nothing shall by any means hurt you."

Picture in your mind you actually having supernatural power and authority over your wounds, where the only evidence of your wound is a healed closed scar in which you use as a testimony to help draw others to a place in God that they, too, may be able to get beyond their wounds. You have just been mentally trained of the awareness of a wound, its purpose, and outcome. This inner insight alone starts the breaking process. Now what you have to remember is where the source of our overcoming power comes from. That is

Jesus Christ. It's by Him that we live, move, and have our being. When we become more aware of His supernatural presence, and the reason of His existence, we then begin the process of sharpening our spiritual tools. The more we read the Word of God, the more we gain strength and power to overcome. It will be soon that you'll begin to see your behavior change as you become a champion of being an overcomer.

Whom the Son (Jesus Christ) has set free is free indeed (John 8:36)!

(Can you speak this in the atmosphere seven times?)

I am free, and I am free indeed in the name of Jesus!

By shouting this in the atmosphere, you are making a declaration and a decree that Jesus Christ has destroyed the power of Satan in your life, and you are no longer bound but rather have been set free. You are now exercising your spiritual authority. Now the healing process can begin because you have acknowledged Jesus as the Great Physician. There is supernatural power and authority in the acknowledgment of Jesus as being our Lord and Savior.

Having been sexually abused as a baby was one of the many of generations of wounds that had fallen on me to stop the plan of God on my life. However, it is through these principles of God that I was able to get beyond my wounds. And it's through applying these principles that you, too, will learn how to get beyond your wounds and truly live.

Note

____

____

____

____

Who's to Blame?

The blame game. Knowing who to blame. Now that you understand that it's not your mother, father, boss, pastor, husband, or any other person or thing that is the culprit to be blamed. We have to be reminded that it's so easy to place the blame of our life issue on some person, place, or thing.

Let's take a look at the blame game that originated with Adam and Eve in Genesis 3:1–4:

> Now the serpent was more subtle than any beast of the field which the Lord had made.

And he (the serpent) said to the woman, Yea, hath God said, Ye shall not eat of every tree of the garden. And the woman said unto the serpent, We may eat of the fruit of the trees of the Garden, but of the fruit of the tree which is in the midst of the garden, God hath said Ye shall not eat of it neither shall Ye touch it, least Ye die. And the serpent said to the women Ye shall not surly die.

Now let's move down to Genesis 3:11–13 where God asked the question:

Hast thou eaten of the tree, wherefore I commanded thee that thou shouldest not eat? And the man said, the woman whom thou gavest to be with me, she gave me of the tree and I did eat. And the Lord God said unto the woman, What is this that thou hast done. And the woman said, The serpent beguiled (enchant in a deceptive way) me and I did eat.

Here we see truly who's to be the blamed. Satan, in disguise, tricked Adam and Eve to disobey that which God had commanded them not to do. The enemy (Satan) will use any possible door opening to bring about affliction and damnation to the children of God. These afflictions brought on by the enemy comes by way of hurt, sickness, disease, disappointment, oppression, depression, stress, aggravation, and frustration. What we must understand is that we cannot be ignorant to the devices of the enemy. We have to be able to identify the works of Satan, even in the smallest areas of a situation. Once this identity is recognized, we then no longer fault that which is seen with only the natural eyes, but rather, we get to the root of the matter and begin to bind and rebuke the works of

Satan, which originated in the spiritual realm first and then manifested in the natural.

2nd Corinthians 2:11 states, "Lest Satan should get an advantage of us: for we are not ignorant to his device."

Being aware of the works and operations of the enemy brings you closer to the truth. You will then realize that Satan is a master of disguise and the father of lies. Now I know some don't believe in Jesus and heaven or in Satan and hell, but they, too, are both real. Good and evil is a reality. You can't be like an ostrich putting your head in the ground and ignoring the knowledge of the kingdom of God and its work and the kingdom of Satan and its works. What we must understand is that which is unseen to the natural eyes does not make it inevitable (unable to avoid).

It is often hard to place the blame on that which one cannot see and easy to place the blame on that which one can see. We have to remember that our enemy, Satan, is a spirit, and a spirit has to embody itself to carry out its will. This is why Satan is known as the master of disguise. The enemy will have to beguile a person in order for them to yield their will over to the enemy, and once this is done, he then uses the individual to carry out his will.

Even though a person has to yield one's will over to the enemy in order for the enemy to use them, we still know who is truly the master at work behind the scenes. This is the purpose why Jesus had to come on earth and suffer, bleed, and die to condemn sin in the flesh. That through the shedding of the blood of Jesus, we can now say that sin no longer has power or dominion over us.

In 1 Thessalonians 5:23, the Word of God says that we are spirit that has a soul that lives in a body.

In order to truly get beyond your wounds, you must always be able to identify the source of which the affliction is coming from. Once you have identified the true source of your affliction, you can now be aware that who you are fighting is not flesh and blood. This is the first form of spiritual awareness. Remember, we are spirit that has a soul that lives in a body.

Satan does not want us to operate in our spiritual form. So we know, as long as we are confined to and only operate in the function of our flesh, we will never be able to defeat or overcome the assignment of the devil in one's life. It is only when we become spiritually aware of Satan and his operations, and counteract by utilizing our spiritual weapons in which God has given to us, it will be then and only then that we become a threat to Satan and his kingdom.

Ephesians 6:12 states, "For we wrestle not against flesh and blood but against principalities, against power, against ruler of the darkness of this world, against spiritual wickedness in high place."

Repeat this prayer out loud.

Spiritual Awakening

Father God, in the Name of Jesus, open up the eyes of my understanding. Give me revelation and knowledge of Your

Word so that I may know who is truly the enemy of my life. Teach me Your Word. Sharpen the gift of discernment on the end inside of me, for Your Word says we wrestle not against flesh and blood but against principalities, against the rulers of the dark-ness of the world, against spiri-tual wickedness in high places. I decree and declare that I'm no longer blinded to that which exists in the spiritual realm.

So we see that the origin of your affliction, hurt, wound, heartaches, and pain was con-structed by Satan himself in the realm of the spirit first. One thing I never did was blame my life issues on someone else, even though I was raised by my mother who was on drugs and mentally unstable and who had been abused herself. We lived in places that were often unstable for anyone to live.

However, I never fault her for that which was done to me as a baby, a child, and a young adult. I always felt that she did the best that anyone could have done, being bounded by their own demon, trying to raise two kids. I can remember being thankful that her drugs and alcohol issues didn't allow her to abandon us. I was her greatest intercessor even at the age of seven, not even knowing anything about God or Jesus but believing that there was a God who could hear my prayer and deliver my mother.

Note

____

____

____

____

Chapter
4

The Weapons of Our Warfare

Let's identify the weapons God has given us to defeat the enemy. In order to identify why our spiritual weapons are needed, you must identify your component. His name is Lucifer, better known as Satan. The Word of God said he was a chief angel, the son of the morning, the minister of music. Satan was dethroned from his seated position in heaven because he said within himself that he would exalt himself over God's throne, that he would ascend above the highest clouds, and that he would be like the Most High God (Isaiah 14:12–17).

For this cause, God dethrone him and told Satan he would be brought down to the lowest depth of the pit. In his anger, Satan convinced a third of the angelic angels to follow him in his attempts to make war against the children of God, God's creations. Do you not know that you are God's creation created in the image of God?

So we see that the battle is not ours but the Lord's. This is why it's important that we know the Word of God and come into the knowledge of our spiritual weapons He has given us to defeat the enemy. What we must understand is that we are all God's creations, created in His image. Let's take a look at Genesis 1:26–27:

> And God said Let us make man in our images after our likeness and let them have dominion over the fish of the sea and over the fowl of the air and over the cattle and over all the earth and over every creeping thing that

creepeth upon the earth. So God created man in his own image, in the image of God created he him; male and female created he them.

Here we see how God has given us spiritual and natural authority to rule and reign victorious through our Lord and Savior, Jesus Christ.

What God has given us is not natural but spiritual. We cannot fight the enemy with the natural weapons of the flesh (anger, lying, hatred, unforgiveness, wrath, envy, murder, strife, high-minded). If you do, you will not win. *You will lose*. We must use the spiritual weapons in which God has given us to win. In the next chapter, we will learn how to apply these spiritual weapons. But for now, let us begin to decree into the atmosphere. 2nd Corinthians 10:4 says, "The weapons of our (My) warfare are not carnal, but might through God."

You have just messed up the enemy's assignment against your life, for you are letting him know that you are spiritually aware of your God-given kingdom weapon. Now that you are beginning to be spiritually aware of your kingdom weapons, you will also begin to be spiritually aware of the devil and his devices by allowing the eye of your understanding to be opened through the Word of God. You are taking the necessary steps on how to use your weapons and the knowledge of your weapon.

These are very powerful tools to the road of your recovery. What will it do a person any good to own a gun but do not know how to use it. Better yet, it does a person no good to own a gun and never practice shooting it because they are afraid of it. Our life, family, happiness, and health depend on us knowing how to use the weapon of our warfare. There are so many spiritual weapons that God has given us, but because these weapons are opposite of the natural weapons that we are familiar with, we tend to let them lie dormant.

God's Spiritual Weapons

The Word of God, prayer, fasting, love, forgiveness, long-suffering, patience.

In my personal life, I've always had people that would judge me due to their own personal issues of jealousy that they needed to be delivered from. I had to learn not to allow my flesh to cause me to retaliate against those in whom I thought wronged me. It is always the enemy's plan to cause one to fight fire with fire or an eye for an eye. Meaning you do me wrong, and I'm going to get you back. These are the uses of natural fleshly weapons. The Lord our God had to teach me on how to use my spiritual weapons that God has given me.

Having the mind of Christ and viewing every situation through the eyes and heart of God will allow you to begin to use your spiritual weapons. You have to begin to exercise the tools that God has given you. Operating in the spirit of love and not retaliating in the flesh was not a benefit to those who hurt me, but rather it was a benefit to myself. By using the spiritual weapons of God, it allowed me to be able to live a life of freedom through my Lord and Savior, Christ Jesus, and not be held in bondage by any.

Note

____

____

____

____

Forgetting Those Things That Are Behind You

Let us look at what it really means to forget those things which are behind you as indicated in Philippians 3:13. For we first have to understand that if God said it, then that settles it. In other words, if God says it can be done, then it can be done. We must get beyond the natural viewing of what the Word of God is saying and begin to review/ see God's Word for what it really is, which is spiritual.

When we look at Philippians 3:13, it reads, "But this one thing that I do, forgetting those things which are behind and reaching forth unto those things which are before." So here we come to understand what the true meaning of the above statement of forgetting is. This statement of forgetting is not referring to remembering it no more, but rather it is referring to the power of its remembrance. The Word of God says that man is body, soul, and spirit. It is the soul part of man which enables him to think and reason, which renders him a subject of moral government. This is why our spirit man has to be born again (John 3:4) so that the soul and the flesh of a man will come subject to the will of God.

Let us take a look at the soul of a man.

We know that our five senses (sight, smell, taste, touch, and hearing) are all connected to the soul of the man and can bring forth memories from the beyond. A familiar smell can bring back old memories of a person, place, or thing, so let's take a look at the above, forgetting as if being erased from your mindset is premature thinking.

Well how do I get to a place as Paul is referring to in the above statement?

You begin to break the source of its remembrance power.

So when the enemy and his demonic darkness shoots by you and brings a familiar thought to remind you of your wounds, hurt, and pain, you immediately cut the source of its power off so that you do not have a natural reaction or effect. Remember, the power of the enemy reminding you of the wounds is so that he may get a human response from you. Most of the time when we are reminded of our past hurt, it often brings forth a change in how you are currently feeling. So if you are feeling happy and joyful, the thought of the hurt and pain that you went through will bring about sadness and depression.

Jesus was our great demonstrator when He allowed the crucifixion to take place. The Word of God says that Jesus learned obedience by the things in which He suffered. Meaning, He never responded in the human flesh. He kept His mouth that it didn't speak bad things, He did not allow His mind to think evil against those who were beating Him, but rather He said, "Father, forgive them for they know not." His will became subject to the will of the living God.

So now when the enemy tries to remind you of your past failures, hurt, and pain, you don't get depressed or oppressed, giving the enemy a natural response. You don't get an attitude with others or get mad with others, giving forth a human response. So what do I do? You begin to bind the thoughts of the enemy, and you begin to open up your mouth and give God the praise. You begin to shout "Hallelujah." You begin to thank the Lord our God for the peace of God that passes all understanding. You break the power of its source and begin to release a spiritual response. The release of the spiritual response, which we will discuss further, will begin to break the strongholds of your mind.

Can we take a moment and put this theory to test? What we are going to do is start praising God. While you are praising God, I want you to notice how your mind will immediately become subject to the praise. You notice how nothing in that moment will take precedence over your praise to God. Meaning that God becomes the center of your thought, your emotions, and your actions.

Come on, Repeat after Me

Father God, in the name of Jesus, I thank You for being the merciful God that You are. I bless Your name. I appreciate Your love for my life. I thank You for this day and Your grace You have given me. I thank You for Your peace, which keeps my heart and mind in right standard with You. I thank You for being my Provider, everything I need is in You. God, You are worthy to be praised. You are worthy to be glorified. God, I thank You for being Lord over my life. God, I lift Your name on high, for You are worthy of the praise, You are worthy of the glory, You are worthy of my hallelujah. This I praise and pray in Jesus's name.

This is a spiritual response that we forget those things which are behind us and begin to press toward that which is before us. Press in praise, press in your worship, press to live and not die! Don't allow the enemy to hold your mind in bondage! Refuse to be held captive in your mind with the pain of the past in which you cannot go back in time to change. Refuse to be held to the grave. Arise, open up your mouth, and begin to exercise your spirit authority. Praise God and be free.

This is how we truly become free of the pain of remembrance and begin to function spiritually as Paul said in Philippians 3:13, "Forgetting those things which are behind, and reaching forth unto those things which are before." Apply this praise exercise when the enemy tries to remind you of your past pain. Apply this praise exercise when trouble arises, and the enemy tries to keep you imprisoned in your mind. Break free and begin to praise and watch the shift take place in your mind.

The spirit of anger illness was a generational curse that had to be broken from my life. I didn't learn of these generations of anger issues that resided in my own family lineage until I was well in my late thirties. But it confirmed many of the issues that I dealt with in my own personal life. However, it is only when I allowed Jesus Christ to come into my life that God taught me how not to allow myself to be trapped in my own mindset with anger and unforgiveness when reminded of my past wound. Having the Spirit of God and the Word of God, you, too, will begin to get beyond your wound and truly operate in the spirit of love, not allowing what you go through in life to hold you in bondage.

Note

The Release of a Spiritual Response

We have to remember that we are spirits and souls. God blew His own Spirit into man, and man became a living soul (Genesis 2:7). Therefore, it is always the enemy's job to cause the children of God to be bound to their own flesh, producing a fleshy response. Remember, the stronger man in you will dominate and override the other. What do I mean by the stronger man? Your spirit or your flesh. Whichever you feed the most, whether it's your flesh or your spirit, it will soon become the stronger man and omit the other one from its full functional operational power.

The release of a spiritual response is simply disciplining our flesh and allowing our spiritual man to arise and dominate the situation and obstacles.

Galatians 5:16 states, "This I say then, walk in the Spirit, and ye shall not fulfill the lust of the flesh."

So how does this work?

In order to release a spiritual response, we must walk in the Spirit. In order to walk in the Spirit, we must first feed our spirit with the Word of God. Matthew 4:4 says, "It is written Man shall not live by bread alone, but by every word that proceeded out of the mouth of God." We must understand that the Word of God is Christ's breath itself, and it alone has spiritual authority and spiritual governmental ranking in which the elements of the spiritual, natural, and human realms must come subject to (Hebrews 4:12).

What we must do is begin daily to eat (read) the Word of God so that our spiritual man is renewed (given divine strength) daily. We will never release a spiritual response if we don't feed our spiritual man. By reading the Word of God daily, it allows our spiritual man to have communications with God, to be instructed by God, and to be led by God who is the Spirit of the Living Word.

Once we begin to allow God to instruct us, we then begin to walk, operate, and talk as spiritual beings. When this begins to take place daily, the flesh loses it power and begins to come subject to the Holy Spirit that is within you. Try training yourself to read a Bible verse a day. You don't have to read a whole chapter at once. And there will be some days you're not going to even feel like reading the Word of God, but try your best to at least read or listen to a Bible verse. It will help you in the long run.

1st John 4:4 states, "We are God, little children and have overcome: because greater is He that is in you, than He that is in the world."

This scripture describes the power that lies within. When we begin to allow the Holy

Ghost that lives within us to be fed with the Word of God daily, and we allow prayer to be fervent in our life, we then begin to tap into the spiritual authority that Christ has given us to be successful spiritually and naturally.

If someone lies on you, talks bad about you, or blaspheme your name, what would be your reaction? It is typical to respond with our flesh. This does not take much effort. Therefore, we have to train our mind, body, soul, and spirit to respond according to the Word of God, which is the will of God for our life. This, of course, takes much denying of our flesh.

You may ask the question, "What do you mean by denying my flesh?"

To deny is the act of refusing to give or grant. In other words, saying no to your flesh. For example, there, put before you, are two plates. One plate has a slice of German chocolate cake on it, and the other has five pieces of carrots and one piece of celery on it. Now, immediately, our fleshly mind says, "Get the cake," and we begin to reach for it, but the spiritual side of us already knows that too much of this kind of eating, "cake eating," will cause obesity and health issues.

So now there is a war within ourselves. Should I? Or should I not? Let's take a look at Romans 7:21, "I find then a law, that when I would do good, evil is present with me." This verse shows us how our born-again spirit (good) and our flesh(bad) is constantly at war with each other. This is why it is so important, the denying of our flesh. The more we deny our flesh, the more we will gain power over it, thereby releasing a spiritual response. We have to be reminded that our flesh always wants its way, but the more we say no to our flesh, the stronger our spiritual man will become.

One of the first things God took from me was smoking, drugs, and alcohol. I was a heavy abuser of alcohol and had been smoking since the age of ten. But it was only when I gave my life to Christ, in my late twenties, that God gave me the willpower to break its power. I can remember it like it was yesterday. God spoke to my spirit, one day, as I was walking to my bedroom, and He said, "Put the cigarette down," meaning, stop smoking them. I was so excited to hear the Lord's voice that I immediately put them down. I had a pack on my dresser, but I did not touch it.

The first day went by without me having a cigarette, and I was okay because I was still under the excitement of hearing the Lord's voice. However, on the second day, the withdrawal symptoms began. I was having chest pains, shortness of breath, and my left arm began to hurt. And I cried out to God, "I can't do it!" He then responded and said, "Give me one more day."

I had to press in faith, believing that on the third day, that through His power, I would be free. This was a breaking of my flesh, and me telling it No! You cannot have a cigarette. On the third day, sure enough, the stronghold of the cigarette broke. This is how we release a spiritual response when we do not allow our flesh to control us. Now don't get me wrong, there's nothing wrong with having help. God graced my husband, and he stopped smoking with the help of a smoking patch. What was required of me was not required of him. God tells us "to much is given, much is required." Meaning that which God had placed in me required immediacy, and He gave me His helping power to overcome it.

Note

____

____

____

____

____

The Emotional Matters

In this chapter, we will understand that our emotions play a series of roles in our walk in life and our walk in Christ. First, we must understand that our emotions do matter. Who wants to be beaten, abused, raped, abandoned, mistreated, talked about, lied on, etc.? No one does! These major things have a great profound effect on our emotions. However, even though our emotions do matter, we cannot, I repeat, we cannot allow our emotional matters to have control over us.

We see all through the Bible how God tells us to love because God is love.

1ˢᵗ Peter 3:8 states, "Finally be ye all of one mind, having compassion one of another, love as brethren, be pitiful, be courteous, not rendering evil for evil or railing for railing: but contrariwise blessing knowing that ye are there unto called that ye should inherit a blessing."

So it's important that we know that our emotions also play a part in our servitude to God. We have to be able to separate the good emotions from the bad ones. God tells us to be compassionate to one another and to love even as Christ loves (Ephesians 5:25).

Knowing the differences between our God-given emotions and the state of our emotional matters will better help us to show forth the true servitude of God. It will also teach us how to spiritually and mentally discern its appearance in all aspects of our lives.

Philippians 4:6 says, "Be careful for nothing: but in everything by prayer and supplication with thanksgiving let your request be made know unto God. And the peace of God, which passeth all understanding, shall keep your heart and mind through Christ Jesus."

If we take a closer look at what the Lord is telling us in the above scripture, we will see how the Lord exposes the spirits that are connected to our emotional matters. Let's take a look at them.

1. First, we see the spirit of anxiousness (being careful for nothing). This spirit will cause one to do or say something out of timing. Due to stress overload attached to the emotions, a lot of people suffer from mental and physical diseases such as high blood pressure, heart disease, mental disorder, extreme fatigue, and many other illnesses because of anxiety.

2. Secondly, we see a worrying spirit. This spirit will cause you not to pray and omit your faith in God's Word. So the Lord tells us in His Word that in everything, we ought to pray. Prayer is an acknowledgment of God and His Word and a reliance that He will answer. Tell yourself, "If I pray, God will answer." God also tells us in His Word that He puts

His Word above His name. This is a very powerful divine gesture. Therefore, it is so important that we speak God's Word openly and verbally. The Word of God says, "We shall decree a thing and it shall be established" (Job 22:28). In other words, we shall demand it in the atmosphere, and it will produce itself in the natural.

3. Therefore it's so important that we don't allow the spirit of worrying to control our thoughts, but rather we should open up our mouths and begin to decree that we are more than conquerors through Jesus Christ who loves us.

When we begin to apply the Word of God in our lives and to situations in our lives, we then take back the control of our emotions and bring them subject to the Word of God. It is very crucial that we don't allow our mind-set (the emotional matter) to conduct and/or control our actions. We see this in the everyday lives of people, when someone has made a person so mad that they allow their emotion to get so far out of control to the point that they're no longer themselves. At that moment, the enemy has taken full control of that person's mind, and that person is a danger to anyone around them, even themselves.

Because of these uncontrolled emotions, many people suffer loss of life, relationships, job, marriage, and divine appointed blessing. This is why the Lord tells us in His Word (1 Peter 1:13), "Gird up the loins of your mind, be sober in your thinking and hope to the end for the grace that is to be brought unto you at the revelation of Jesus Christ." A sober mind-set produces a godly and rational behavior conduct. Therefore, you are in control of your emotions in situations and circumstances. So you have to tell yourself, "I will not allow people, places, or things to get me to act out the deeds of my flesh." Sometimes you have to settle your mind. In other words, you have to silence your thoughts and allow the peace of God to rule in your heart.

I can remember being hurt so badly to the point that I almost allowed my emotions to cause me to walk away from the assignment in which God, Himself, called me to do. I had to learn how to control my emotions. Remember, as I stated above, if a person allows the enemy to run rapid in their emotions and agree with him, he can cause them to do bodily harm to someone or act out fatal actions causing themselves to be put in jail or worse. The Word of God tells us to be quick to hear, slow to speak, and slow to wrath. Never allow yourself to make a major move when you are upset or when you are angry.

Now it is also important to know that one's emotions are not only manifested through being angry or upset. A person can be tired and become weary in well-doing, and their emotions can kick in, allowing them to move out of the will of God or make drastic decisions. These are times when one needs to take a step back and allow God to have full control of the situation. Sometimes this can be hard, but if you begin to train your emotions, you will then begin to see the hand of God move in your life. We see this also in the Prophet Elijah when he got tired, and he allowed his flesh to cause him to give up on that which God had called him to do (1 Kings 19).

Note

Knowing Who You Are

It's so important that you know who you are, and who the Word of God says you are. We are more than conquerors through Jesus Christ that loves us. This is a powerful word given to us by God Himself. To conquer means to overcome and to take control. So let's take a step back and really look at what lies within us. We have the power within us to be able to succeed in dealing with any problem.

I have seen people hinge their life and deliverance on others feeling sorry for them. What do you mean? For example, you hear some say, "You don't know my life story. You don't know what I've been through. You don't know how badly I was hurt. You don't under-stand how they talked about me. You don't know how they mistreated me." This can go on and on and on. Self-seeking sympathy does not validate who you are as a person. It only prolongs your deliverance.

This is the patting or pacifying of the flesh, which cradles low self-esteem and imprisons you to a quick moment of feeling good. Once the quick fix feeling is worn off, you will go right back to a place of seeking man's sympa-thy and approval. This will go on and cause one to lose focus of who they really are. Now it is okay to allow someone to encourage you, motivate you, mentor you, and assist you to where you would like to be in life, but never allow them to take the place of God in your life. Don't worship them to the point that you are codependent on them.

Remember, you're more than a conqueror. You have to know who you are and who you belong to. Tell yourself, "I am the daughter or son of the Most High God. I am beauti-ful and wonderfully made. I am strong, I am powerful, I am smart with the wisdom and knowledge of God." You see, it does not matter the difference of how anyone views you. Once you know who you are in Christ, you will begin to fuel your inner man and, now, instead of looking for self-encouragement, you can be the encourager. How great and beautiful is that.

Now let's get a greater understanding. Just because you know who you are in Christ, this does not mean that you are operating in the spirit of pride, as some would say. No, what it means is that you have become spiritually aware and spiritually confident in who you are in God. You have become functional in faith and the substance of the hope that you have in the sovereign God that you serve. This also means that you understand the spiritual weapon that has been given to you for the work of the kingdom of God.

So let's stop for a moment and do an exercise.

Close your eyes, and for a moment, we are going to forget about those things that are behind you (Philippians 3:13)—stress, pain, aggregation, frustration, anger, failure. Breathe in through your nose and slowly exhale through your mouth. After you exhale, repeat, "I am more than a conqueror through Jesus Christ who loves me." Do this three times.

Begin to tell yourself daily that Jesus Christ loves me. Not only do you have to know that Jesus loves you, but you have to love yourself as well. When you don't know who you are, you will allow the enemy to use people and/or circumstances to devalue who you are. We see this in a lot of abusive relationships. You have to know that you are powerful and are wonderfully made by God.

Paul said in Philippians 3:18, "That He forgetting those things which are behind him and reaching forth unto those things which are before." We have to understand that greatness is before us, but you will never obtain it if you allow your past to imprison you. Begin to use that conquering power that God has placed in you. So reach, stretch, and push toward that which God promised you, that which you deserve because you are worth it.

I have had my character attacked. I have been made fun of for how I look, and this was not by those who were in the world. I had to learn how not to change who I am to please people. I am a visual person, a seer, and when I would teach and preach God's Word, I would see what God was saying, and I would deliver it hands on. You have heard some say that they are a hands-on person, meaning they receive and learn instructions hands on. Well, sometimes, this was not approved by man. So I tried to do it their way (change), and it always felt as if I was performing to please the person, which allowed confusion to come in because I didn't want to appear as disobedient.

This is when God stepped in and said, "Stop." He told me, "I made you different. You will never be as the norm. Continue to allow me to use you as I choose to. You have to understand that some people will never see the good in what you do, even if the change is made to fit their personal purpose. Therefore, you must understand that this is not your problem. It is the individual's own personal issues that they need to be delivered from. Learn to love who you are. Don't conform yourself to what people want you to be. Be who God has called you to be through the renewing of your mind daily through the Word of God. Allow God to groom you to the person He wants you to be."

A lot of times, we are already that person. We just need to be cleaned up from our old doings. So be ye thankful. Love yourself and appreciate the person who God has made you to be.

Note

____

____

____

The Challenging Times

What we will learn in this chapter is how to remain stable, positive, and focused during challenging times. A lot of the time, challenging times come in unexpected moments. Most times we are usually caught off guard, shocked, and amazed, wondering, *How did this happen?* Or *How did I get to this place?* When we feel that we're at our strongest or when things seem to be just going our way, these are the moments when the enemy (Satan) brings forth sneak attacks. The mind tends to race when problems occur. We forget that we have a Savior. We also forget the basic fundamentals of our peace, hope, strength, and our courage. Everything we have been through, even if it's through self-encouragement, usually goes out the window when challenging times appear.

How can I be victorious during challenging times?

Notice that when things are going okay and fine, and then all of a sudden, *bam*, trouble, trials, and/or tribulations arise. Now, all day you're troubled in your mind and spirit, wrestling inwardly with things, people, or problems that are beyond what you can change or resolve. The Word of God tells us to cover our heads with the helmet of salvation. Notice that a helmet is used as a form of protection in combat. First Peter 1:13 tells us to gird up the loins of our mind. In other words, stop allowing the enemy from hijacking our thoughts. If we don't stop our minds from repeatedly replaying a bad situation, we will be trapped in a time loop, allowing our thoughts to torment us with the challenges of that moment.

So the Word of God tells us that we have to think soberly (Roman 12:3).

Now picture a person under the influence of alcohol and/or drugs. What do you see? I see a person who is impaired in their thinking. When you are under the influence of the enemy, you will be controlled by the enemy. Most people that are under the heavy influence of drugs and alcohol, you will see the signs of the influence. They will have some kind of slurred speech, walking imbalance, forefront actions, mood swings, etc. Let's take a look at some of the influences of a challenging time.

One tends to worry, be upset, frustrated, impatient, aggravated, spontaneous outbursts, mad, and have mood swings. So now what we have to do is to take back control of our life in challenging times. This is why God tells us that we must gird up the loins of our mind. Girding up your mind is a form of action you take to silence the voice of your mind. Once this is done, you can begin to think on things that are lovely, just, honest, and of a good report in which the Word of God says these are the things we should be thinking on. You don't have to be bound by your thought. Train yourself in challenging times to change the way you are thinking. We have to know that there is a Higher Power on our side, which is Jesus Christ, our Lord and Savior. So this lets us know we are not alone.

All things work together for the good of them that love the Lord to them who are called according to His purpose. God has called us all into His kingdom. We just have to acknowledge Jesus as our Lord and Savior and begin to thank God for the things He has already done for you. For example, waking you up; keeping you from all hurt, harm and danger; protecting and covering your children. These are things that God does for us. We should acknowledge its working power in our life daily. Begin to speak the Word of God over your life. Knowing that whatever your current challenge is, God will see you through. Speaking positively over your life keeps you in the protection of God.

Every morning, when I wake up, I begin to decree and declare over my life, my children's lives, and my husband's life. This allows me to stay close to God by acknowledging Him as my protector. So when challenging times arise, even if it's been permitted by God, I know that God is with me to see me through. God told us in His Word that He will never leave nor forsake us, that He would be with us even to the end of time. So by applying the above principles it allows one to keep God at the forefront of their mind and heart. Now this will make it hard for the enemy to try to get you out of the will of God. This we see, again, how focused Jesus was when He had to take the journey to His crucifixion. He understood it had to take place, but He also knew that the Father was in Him. So He was not caught off guard when challenging times presented itself.

Say this out loud, "Lord, shift my attention on You. Help me to stay grounded and true to Your Word even in challenging times. Let my flesh not arise, but remind me that You are here daily with me to fight for me."

Applying these applications are easier said than done. But with continual discipline in practicing these applications, you will soon be able to do what the Word of God says. "Standing and having done all to stand."

Note

10

Daily Maintenance

I want to testify that getting beyond your wound will not happen overnight. But I am a living testimony that if you apply what you have learned in this book, you will surely get to a place in your life that you are not bound by your past or your current situation. Life goes on, and you must learn how to appreciate every moment and make the moment worth living, even when things are not going our way. Life is worth living.

The Word

The Word is so important to our deliverance. We cannot do anything on our own. We need the power of His Word. We should always have a Bible on hand. Bible apps are really good as well. When you need a "right now" word for a situation that you may be in, you can type it into the Bible app, and it will bring it right up. For example, say someone made you upset or angry. You can type in the word *anger*, and it will bring up all scriptures pertaining to that. Then you begin to read them and let the Word of God minister to your spiritual man. You can look up words like *fatigue, worrying,* and *joy*. Whatever you need counseling in at that moment, you will find it in the Word of God. Do this daily. Once you begin to remember the Word of God, you will likely refer back to it in any situation and/ or circumstance.

Prayer

This is one of my favorite tools that I use daily. So what is prayer? Prayer is first the acknowledgment of God and Jesus Christ as our Lord and Savior.

For example, "Jesus, I acknowledge You as being my Lord and Savior. I thank You, Father God, for being my Provider. Thank You for being the Waymaker, making ways out of no ways. Thank You for being my Protector." We have to learn and train ourselves to be careful of nothing but everything by prayer and supplication (Philippians 4:6–8). Every morning, begin to acknowledge God through the name of Jesus, and you will start receiving the benefits that come along with its acknowledgment. Do this periodically during the course of the day. Just begin to say, "Thank You, Jesus."

Applications of the Word

Begin to apply the Word in your life. If the Word of God says the joy of the Lord is your strength, in order for this word to be applied, the word will be tested within you. That means something will cause you to get upset, and at that moment, you will have to begin to remind yourself that you have power over that thing and begin to allow the joy of the Lord to consume and overtake that problem.

Another example: The Word of God says love your enemies. Oh, wow! You can feel the resistance in the flesh. Well, guess what? In order for you to apply this word, heads up. You already know that someone will do something that will cause your flesh to want to shut down and then distance yourself to have nothing else to do with that person. But the Word of God says we have to love them, even as He loves us daily (Matthew 5:44).

What we have to understand is that we become stronger and powerful when we allow the Word of God to have full reign in our life. God will come and test His Word in us, just to see if it is stable (has root and foundation). The enemy (Satan) will also come and tempt God's Word in you, just to see if you yourself believe in the depth of it. This is the trying of our faith (James 1:3–4). So we understand that it is important to do a daily maintenance in ourselves so that we can not only practice what we proclaim but proclaim that which we have practiced. You can do this one day at a time. Challenge yourself daily to say, "I will be all that God would have me to be, according to His Word."

In closing, know that God loves you. And there is nothing you can do to stop His love for you. God wants to see you happy. He says, "I know the thoughts that I have of you, good thoughts to give you the expected end" (Jeremiah 29:11, paraphrased).

Note

About the Author

Nicole Haynes was born in Amityville, New York. While still a young child, her mother moved her and her brother to Florida. Being anointed by God from the womb as His called prophetess, the enemy immediately sent out an attack on her life. These demonic attacks involved being molested as an infant, born into generations of curses of alcohol, drugs, and so much more. At the age of seven, having to watch her mother being bound by her own wounds of molestation, drugs, and alcohol abuse, it was then that the anointing of spiritual intercessional prayer began to be ignited upon her.

During those times as a young child, she began to pray for her mother that God would deliver her from her own demons of affliction. Knowing nothing about Christianity or God, but within herself knowing that there was a God, she began to immaturely tap into the spiritual realm of prayer. She believes it was during this time that the enemy began to intensify spiritual warfare on her life. Drugs and alcohol by the age of eleven, dropping out of school at the age of fourteen, pregnant at the age of fifteen—things began to spiral out of control fast. It was at the age of twenty-five that God made His official visitation to her to confirm His hand and calling upon her life.

From that point on, God began to anoint her and train her to be the curse-breaker and to be able to live the blessed life that has been ordained by God unto her. Although this came by great submission and obedience to God, her life has never been the same. One who has overcome difficult personal challenges as well as a hostile destructive environment, now she had been graced by God to use those learning experiences and valuable spiritual tools to empower, mentor, and teach others as well to excel beyond their wounds.